Chatterbox

For Margie, Peter and Gwennie – MW

For Claudine and Lachlan – DN

PUFFIN BOOKS

UK | USA | Canada | Ireland | Australia
India | New Zealand | South Africa | China

 Penguin
Random House
Australia

Penguin Random House Australia is part of the Penguin Random House group of companies
whose addresses can be found at global.penguinrandomhouse.com

First published by Penguin Group (Australia), 2006
This paperback edition published by Penguin Group (Australia), 2008

Text and cover design by Tony Palmer © Penguin Random House Australia
Illustrations by Deborah Niland
Typeset in 22pt Perpetua
Printed and bound in China

A catalogue record for this
book is available from the
National Library of Australia

ISBN 978 0 14 350161 9

Penguin Random House Australia uses papers that are natural and recyclable products,
made from wood grown in sustainable forests. The logging and manufacture processes
are expected to conform to the environmental regulations of the country of origin.

penguin.com.au

chatterbox

Margaret Wild

Illustrated by

Deborah Niland

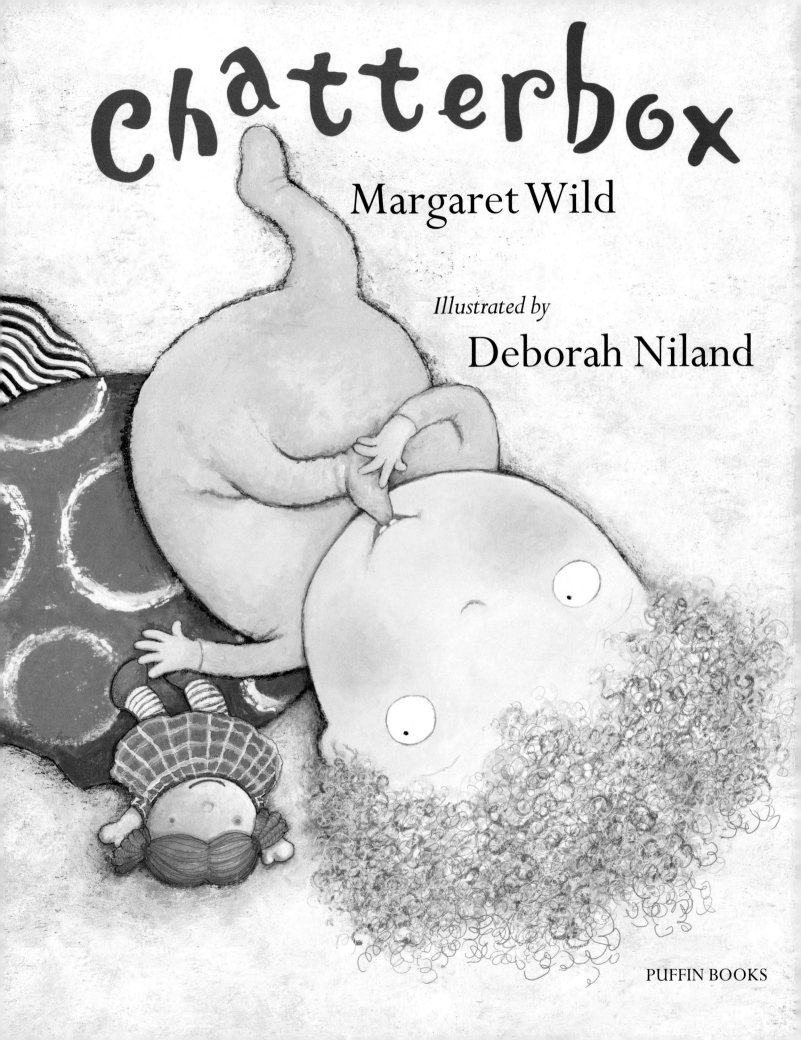

PUFFIN BOOKS

Max's baby sister, Daisy, was gorgeous.

She twiddled her toes.

She crawled.

She played with
cardboard boxes.

She splashed in the bath.

She built towers
out of blocks.

She listened to stories.

She banged on pots and pans.

She did everything
except talk.

'Daisy dear, say *Mama*,' said Mum.

'Daisy darling, say *Dada*,' said Dad.

'Daisy sweetheart, say *Nana*,' said Nana.

'Please, Daisy, say *Max*,'
said Max. '*Max-Max-Max!*'

But Daisy just sucked her dummy, and said nothing.

'When is she going to talk?' asked Max. 'When?'

But no one knew.

They took Daisy to Pet Day at Max's school.
'Daisy dear, say *woof*,' said Mum.
'Daisy darling, say *miaow*,'
said Dad.

'Daisy sweetheart, say *tweet*,'
said Nana.
'Please, Daisy, say *squeak*,'
said Max. '*Squeak-squeak-squeak!*'

But Daisy just stuck her bottom in the air, and said nothing.

They took Daisy for a holiday in the country.
'Daisy dear, say *moo*,' said Mum.

moo

'Daisy darling, say *neigh*,' said Dad.

neigh

'Daisy sweetheart, say *baa*,'
said Nana.

baa

'Please, Daisy, say *quack*,'
said Max. '*Quack-quack-quack!*'

quack

quack

quack

But Daisy just blew a spit bubble, and said nothing.

'Daisy sweetheart, say *hoot*,'
said Nana.

hoot

'Please, Daisy, say *snap*,' said Max.
'*Snap-snap-snap!*'

snap
snap
snap

grrr

But Daisy just ate a banana, and said nothing.

woof

'When is she going to talk?' asked Max. 'When?'
But no one knew.

miaow

squeak

Then, one morning, at breakfast,
Daisy put down her spoon.

She opened her mouth,
and she said,

'Mama dear, Dada darling,
Nana sweetheart,
Max-Max-Max.
Woof, miaow, tweet, squeak-squeak-squeak.
Moo, neigh, baa, quack-quack-quack.
Grrr, ssss, hoot, snap-snap-snap.'

Mum and Dad and Nana and Max stared at Daisy.
They opened their mouths to speak,
but there was no stopping Daisy!

She said,

'Dada, my nappy is soggy and needs changing.'

'Nana, I quite like porridge, as long as it's not lumpy.'

miaow

woof

'Mama, please don't dress me in pink.
I prefer purple.
Max, we can play all afternoon now because
a morning nap is quite enough
for someone my age . . .'

'Daisy . . .?!'

Mum and Dad and Nana and Max tried again to speak,
but there was no stopping Daisy! She said,

'Why is the sky blue, and what makes the wind?'

'Where do stars go in the day,
and how do caterpillars turn
into butterflies?'

'Why is the sea salty, and how do fish breathe underwater?'

Max popped a spoonful of porridge into Daisy's mouth.
'When is she going to stop talking?' he asked. 'When?'

Daisy popped a slice of toast into Max's mouth.

'Never,' she said.

'Never, ever, ever, ever, ever, ever...

...ever!'